P9-AGU-440

DAVID STEVENS. Photograph by Robert Green.

DAVID STEVENS is the author of the play *The Sum of Us*, which ran in New York for a year and won the Outer Critics Circle Award. He also wrote the screenplay for the film.

An Australian citizen, he was born in Palestine of British parents, was brought up in Africa and the Middle East and has worked, intermittently, as a barman, a mortuary assistant and a strip club barker in Kings Cross. His preferred method of travel is by cargo boat.

He wrote the television mini-series of Alex Haley's *Queen*, and when Alex Haley died, David Stevens took over the task of completing the novel of the same name. He directed the mini-series *A Town Like Alice* and was co-author, with Jonathan Hardy and Bruce Beresford of the screenplay *Breaker Morant*. His many credits include writing and directing the mini-series *Always Afternoon* and *A Thousand Skies* and he directed the cult move *The Clinic* as well as two feature films, *Undercover*, and in the U.S.A., *Kansas*. He has recently written a sequel to *The Thorn Birds* mini-series, and has completed a novel about Lawrence of Arabia.

David Stevens presently lives in the French West Indies.

the sum of us
david stevens

CURRENCY PRESS • SYDNEY

First published in 1995 by
Currency Press Ltd
PO Box 452, Paddington NSW 2021, Australia

National Library of Australia
Cataloguing-in-Publication data

    Stevens David, 1940-
      The sum of us.
      ISBN 0 86819 441 7.
      1. Title. II. Title: Sum of Us (Motion picture).
      (Series: Currency film scripts).
    A822.3

Printed by Griffin Colour, Netley, South Australia
Cover design by Susan Mikulic

PUBLISHER'S NOTE: this is the reading script and includes only those camera directions which are essential to the story.

Contents

To LOREN BOOTHBY – FOR LOVE.

Write About What You Know

David Stevens

The play *The Sum of Us* was born out of a complexity of emotions. It came to me at a time when I was deeply lonely, concerned about AIDS, and wanting to write something that expressed my abiding love for Australia.

When I wrote it, I think I knew that I was coming to a crossroads in my life, and I had a nagging suspicion that the direction I would take would lead me away from Australia. At the same time, I learned that three of my three closest friends were HIV Positive, and one was already ill with AIDS, and I wanted to do something, write something, shout something, to express my feelings about this fell disease.

In ways that I don't understand, my reactions to Australia were mixed up in this. It is called 'The Lucky Country', and for me that has been true. Australia has been extraordinarily kind to me. Before I went to Australia I was warned that they didn't like Poms and that they hated poofters, but if that is/was true, I surely didn't find it. There are exceptions to every rule, of course, and Australia has it's share of poofter bashers, but luckily, I didn't meet too many of them. Instead, I met a tolerant people, who responded with kindness and honesty if you were honest with them. And I met a number of Australians (and New Zealanders), who were parents of gay friends and who had made the difficult journey of accepting their children's sexuality, and made them and their lovers welcome in their homes. I watched the responses of some of these parents to the news that their sons were HIV Positive, and again, except in a few circumstances, I saw only love and a deep need to nurture. It is about people such as these that I wanted to write.

But my own loneliness was the direct springboard for the play. Late one night, I had just finished writing a mini-series, *Always Afternoon*, and would deliver it the following day. This is always a difficult time for me, and, I'm sure, many writers. Having created these characters, lived with them, made them one's family, to part with them – to send them off into the big bad world of producers, casting directors, executives – is a wrenching experience.

I sat in my garden in St Kilda, got very drunk, and remembered a woman I had seen once on a train going from Melbourne to Sydney. The woman, drunk in the club car, looked like the loneliest person I had ever seen, and suddenly I wanted to write about her. I went to my computer and wrote a speech describing her. I did not intend to write a play. It was only when I re-read the speech the following morning that the possibility of a larger future for it took hold. Eventually, that speech became the end of the first act. In the movie it's still there, but highly truncated.

I had a speech but no characters, and certainly no plot. Slowly, over the next few months, the piece began to form in my mind, and when the production of *Always Afternoon* was postponed I took time off, locked to door to my house, and let my heart, mind and typing fingers take me where they would.

I think it was the happiest three months of my life. Among other things, I was determined to write a 'pure' play: that is, one that is specific to the theatre, not something that could as easily be written for any other medium.

The theatre is my home, my training ground and my gymnasium. I had the good fortune, when I was a young man in London, to work with the brilliant English director John Dexter, in the days of the 'kitchen sink revolution' at the Royal Court Theatre. They were exciting times. Brecht was the bible, and social revolution was the creed. These lessons stayed with me, and since then I have always believed that the best work is that which aspires, no matter how lightly, to have a social context.

Because I wasn't writing for anyone else, for money or to a deadline, or even in any real hope that the play would ever be produced, a certain perversity took hold of me. I knew that 'Dad' would be a contentious character for some. I knew that people would say that such a tolerant father could not possibly exist, but I had met such fathers, and celebrated them. And Jeff, whose 'normalcy' has upset some people, is based on a number of young men I knew in Melbourne.

Dad's last scene, of course, is my metaphor for AIDS. When the play was written – and I'm sure even now – many people believed AIDS to be a 'gay plague' and that 'it's their own fault.' It isn't a gay plague. Its origins, in Africa, are exclusively heterosexual, and it isn't 'their own fault.' Who knew? Who could possibly have guessed? In order to try and blunt such negativity towards gays, I wanted to invert the syndrome. Instead of the young homosexual being the one who gets sick and has to be looked after, it is the healthy heterosexual who gets sick and has to be looked after. I am my brother's keeper. Or my father's. Or my son's. Or my friend's.

I didn't show the play to anyone when it was finished. I hugged it, my love song to Australia, to my chest, and it was some time before I let even my closest friends read it. Their reactions were sufficiently encouraging to persuade me to send it to a couple of producers, but the response was 'Nice try, Davy, better luck next time,' and so I took my play back, put it in my bottom drawer, and accepted the fact that it would never be performed.

Shortly afterwards, I left Australia to work in the U.S. My agent wanted to see examples of my other writing, and so I showed him the play. I was safe. If it wasn't going to be done in Australia, there was no chance it would be done in the U.S.! To my surprise he sold the play within the week.

Dorothy Lyman, the brave and adventurous producer who was then running 'A DIRECTOR'S THEATRE' in Los Angeles, put her hand up. She dipped into her own pocket, staged the play at a small theatre at USC the next summer, and despite sizzling temperatures, a tin roof and no air conditioning, the play did well.

It was during this production that we had the first of what proved to be many emotional encounters provoked by the play. A young man came to see the play – three times. He talked to us and said that his parents couldn't handle his sexuality, and he wanted to fly them in from Chicago to see the play. Would we meet them afterwards?

The parents came, and afterwards the young man brought them to us. The mother, clearly moved by the play, talked to Dorothy Lyman. The father came to me, shook my hand and said, 'thank you.' Then he put his arm around his gay son's shoulders, and led him away to talk quietly, kindly, gently, affectionately to him.

At around this point, someone, I'm still not sure who, showed a copy of the script to the New York Producer/Director, Kevin Dowling, who flew out to California to see it, and bought the stage and screen rights the next day.

Kevin has been the play's best friend ever since. He produced and directed it the following year at the Williamstown Theatre festival, and the year after that at the Cherry Lane Theatre in New York. And he demanded that I write the screenplay. Half your luck, I said. It can't be adapted to a movie. But Kevin insisted, and so I jumped in. if only to prove him wrong and myself right. It didn't quite work out like that.

It wasn't easy. I didn't know how to handle in cinematic terms all the things I had done as specifically theatrical effects, and after several anguished conversations with Kevin, I decided that it didn't matter. I would write a first draft the way I saw it, and if they didn't like it they could sack me and get another writer. So I tried to re-visualise the piece as a 'pure' movie, in much the same was that I had tried to visualise it as a 'pure' play. I wanted to explore the possibilities of playing around with the cinematic form of playing with time (Grandma), and talking to the audience (Dad and Jeff). It comes directly from my training in Brechtian drama. Brecht never allows you to forget that you are in a theatre, so the emotional effects are hard won. I believe the same can be true of cinema. Whenever I'm in a cinema, I never forget that fact. There's an Italian horror film, starring, I think, Boris Karloff. The last shot is Karloff on horseback riding through a thunderstorm. The camera pulls back to show that the horse is wooden and on rollers, the stormy sky is back projection, and the lightning is an electrician's effect. I loved it.

Is the work 'autobiographical'? No. And Yes.

The story of the grandmother and her female lover of forty years is my grandmother. The Woman on the Train was my experience. Many of the things that the characters say and do are mine or things I have said or experienced. But I am not a working class, heterosexual Australian father, nor a twenty-four-year old rugby playing plumber, and I certainly never had the relationship with my father that Jeff has with his.

But I am reminded of the advice – truism or cliche – often given to young writers. 'Write about what you know.' I am not a young writer, but *The Sum of Us* is what, at that moment in my life, I knew.

Saint Martin, French West Indies
March 1995

Uncomplicated, Honest and 'Right'

Hal McElroy

When I first read the play, *The Sum of Us*, I cried. As a film producer with twenty years under my belt, I'm not easily moved to tears by the written word, but David's writing was so beautifully uncomplicated, honest and 'right' for the characters. But most of all, it is life affirming. I found it absolutely irresistible.

At that moment, I decided I had to make a movie of the play. However, I discovered that someone else had exactly the same idea and was already working with David on a screenplay in New York. That man was Kevin Dowling, who had just produced and directed the play in a very successful Off Broadway production at the Cherry Lane Theatre. At David's urging, I rang Kevin in America, and after an hour or so on the phone – even though we had never met – proposed that we work together to try and get the film made.

Raising finance for a film is an excrutiatingly difficult process and Kevin had already spent fruitless months trying to interest Hollywood in the project. He was delighted to be joined by a partner, but neither of us realised that we'd spend another two years together before we would actually shoot a foot of film.

Dealing with rejection is something a producer must learn very quickly, but the rejection we faced with *The Sum of Us* was unusual. It was constant. No one ever mentioned the word homosexuality, they just said 'no' a thousand different ways. As Kevin and I wrestled with Hollywood financiers, agents, managers and stars, the casting alternatives pushed the budget up and down like a yo-yo. Of all the combinations we put to them, none seemed to be the perfect one to trigger the financing in America until eventually, we said, 'What the hell! Let's make it just as it's written – as a small Australian film, with Jack Thompson as Harry and Russell Crowe as his son Greg.' And that's exactly what we did.

11

We found Australian funding from Southern Star and the Film Finance Corporation and we set the film in Sydney because it has a strong homosexual community in the inner city and a generally tolerant attitude in the community at large.

Shot in thirty days in October/November 1993 with a budget of just over $3.5 million, Kevin Dowling and his co-director and cinematographer Geoff Burton, made what I believe will be remembered as an Australian classic. A working class film about ordinary people, dealing with an extraordinary situation in a most matter of fact way. A film filled with honesty, love and compassion. A film just like I imagined it would be after my first reading three years before.

David's script is the most simple script I've ever produced. There is not a single superfluous word. His stage directions, scene description and dialogue notes are incredibly brief, but absolutely perfect. I asked David how many drafts he had written before the play was ready, as he had done just three re-writes for the screenplay. He replied that some scenes were the result of many different versions, polished, edited and re-written to make right. But with many scenes, the dialogue that appeared in the final draft was just as he wrote it the very first time.

The dialogue has a rhythm of its own. It doesn't necessarily run in a straight, dramatically 'correct' line. It meanders, circles, and refers back, before plunging on to its conclusion. To the eye and the ear, it's absolutely perfect: hilariously funny, and believable.

Everyone associated with the making of *The Sum of Us* is very proud of the end result. It's a lesson in tolerance, and a lesson we can all learn from.

Sydney, April 1995

MAIN CAST (in order of appearance)

Harry Mitchell	JACK THOMPSON
Jeff Mitchell	RUSSELL CROWE
Greg	JOHN POLSON
Joyce Johnson	DEBORAH KENNEDY
Young Jeff	HOSS MORONEY
Gran	MITCH MATHEWS
Mary	JULIE HERBERT
Jenny	REBEKAH ELMALOGLOU
Greg's Mother	SALLY CAHILL
Greg's Father	BOB BAINES

Production Company, Southern Star
Produced by Hal McElroy
Screenplay by David Stevens
Directed by Kevin Dowling and Geoff Burton

Complete film credits appear at the end of the book.

PRINCIPAL CHARACTERS

HARRY MITCHELL, Captain of a Sydney Harbour ferry.
JEFF MITCHELL, his son, a plumber.
GREG, Jeff's friend, a gardener.
JOYCE JOHNSON, Harry's friend.
YOUNG JEFF
GRAN, Harry's mother.
MARY, Gran's partner.
JENNY, Joyce's daughter.
GREG'S MOTHER
GREG'S FATHER

SETTING

The film was made in Sydney and takes place in Harry and Jeff's house in Balmain, an inner-city suburb on the harbour; the Botanic Gardens, pubs and clubs and various other locations around Sydney.

1. B & W FOOTAGE. EXT. DAY (1978)

YOUNG JEFF, aged eight, is playing football with his GRAN and his COUSINS in the backyard at GRAN's house. GRAN, is sixty-ish and fairly butch. MARY, who is GRAN's age, is reading on the porch.

JEFF: The first time Dad took me to Gran and Aunt Mary's for my holiday, I was maybe...I don't know – eight or nine. And I remember playing footy with Gran and my cousins in the front yard. You know those days, when everything's perfect? It was one of the greatest afternoons of my life...You see, Gran would form us all into one team and she'd be the other...It amazes me to think of the hours she'd spend playing with us and she never seemed tired....And later in the afternoons she'd play Ludo or Snakes n' Ladders or tiddly-winks. I used to love those games with Gran. She used to keep an old Monopoly set hidden under the stairs because Mary wouldn't let her play it...Real strict Salvation Army, Mary was...I mean Gran too, but you know, not as bad as Mary. But this one time, Mary went out...for a while and the minute she was out the door Gran got out the old Monopoly board, her eyes all glinting. 'Not a word to Mary', she said. It was the best game of Monopoly I've ever played. My Gran and me were doing something really naughty – really wrong. [*Laughing*] Fire and brimstone stuff, you know...Well some people might think those days with Gran and Mary had a bad influence on me...

2. EXT. FOOTBALL GAME – PRESENT DAY. JEFF IS NOW TWENTY-FOUR.

Footballers are in a scrum on a football field while COACH stands behind them, urging them on. JEFF's head is seen peeking between TWO FOOTBALLERS in a scrum.

JEFF: [*voice over*]... could be right... after all, I still play footy.

COACH: Stick ... your frigging shoulder ... in his arse!

JEFF: Hey, ohh.

FOOTY PLAYER: Watch it!

JEFF: Only doing what he wants.

A FOOTBALLER runs and drop kicks the ball, JEFF pushes the other players out of the way and picks up the loose ball. Another player tackles him as the rest of the team runs in and all jump on top of him.

COACH: Jesus, you...blokes! What the hell do you think you're doing? Come on! Oh, go on, get out of here. Go on!

TITLE IN: THE SUM OF US.

JEFF and FOOTBALLERS jog up the stairs beside the grandstand, along a pathway and out the gate.

3. EXT. DAY. FERRY WHARF

The ferry approaches the wharf. DAD, at the wheel, guides the ferry in with practised ease. The DECKHAND is on deck with rope in hand as the ferry glides beside the jetty. DAD, still in his uniform, leaves the ferry, crosses the street and walks into a corner pub.

4. INT. DAY. PUB

Inside the pub, he joins GERTIE at the bar.

GERTIE: G'day, mate.

They look at a newspaper advertisement that reads: 'COMPUTER DATING Desiree's Introduction Agency. The Modern Alternative'.

DAD: You're a woman of the world, Gert, What do you reckon?

GERTIE: You thinking of getting hitched again, Harry?

DAD: Just looking.

5. EXT. TITLES OVER – DAY

JEFF and FOOTBALLERS are jogging along the street.

6. EXT. TITLES OVER – DAY

DAD, bag in hand, crosses the street to his house, passing NEIGHBOUR *with three greyhounds.*

7. EXT. TITLES OVER – DAY

JEFF and FOOTBALLERS *are jogging through the park.* JEFF *jogs along the street and around the corner into his house, closing the front door after him.*

8. INT. DAD AND JEFF's HOUSE.

DAD is preparing mashed potatoes on the stove. His body wriggles as he stirs the pot. JEFF *stumbles to a chair and sits, breathing heavily. He removes his cap and tosses it onto the floor. He then goes into the kitchen and makes his way to the fridge, passing DAD at the stove.*

JEFF: [*to the camera*] I'm fucked.
DAD: What was that?
JEFF: I said I'm rooted.
DAD: Stopped off for a quickie on the way home, did you?
JEFF reaches into the fridge and takes out two beers, walks over to the
    stove and hands DAD a beer. He looks into the open oven.
JEFF: God, you're off sometimes. You know that? Put a dirty meaning
    on everything. Not lasagna again? Are you going senile or something?
DAD: Mashed potatoes and vegies.
JEFF: Three times this week, already. Why can't we have a nice leg of
    lamb? We haven't had a roast for yonks.
DAD: Things aren't so wonderful when you're cooking, you know.
    Sausages and chips are a real treat when you're in the kitchen.
JEFF: I did that nice chicken curry last week.
DAD: So hot it blew the roof of my mouth off.

JEFF: Oh gee, I'm sorry you can't stand some imagination with my cooking. I'll stick to frozen lasagna from now on. How long's it going to be anyway?

DAD: Nearly ready.

JEFF: I'll grab a quick shower.

DAD: Why do you always decide to take a shower just as I'm about to dish up? Just as I'm about to put the food on the table -

JEFF: You don't expect me to sit down all sweaty and smelly like this, do you?

DAD: Why not? Doesn't usually bother you, unless you're going out. Are you, going out?

JEFF: As a matter of fact I am. I just thought I'd pop down to the pub for a couple of beers. All right?

DAD: Got a date?

JEFF: Can't a bloke go out for a drink on a Friday night without you making a lifetime romance out of it? You dish up and I won't be two ticks, all right?

DAD: [*to camera*] He'll be back in a minute.

JEFF undresses in the bathroom. He tosses his clothes into the adjoining room, notices the shower is dripping and returns to the kitchen wearing only a towel.

JEFF: You had a shower then, did you Dad?

DAD: Yes. Yes, I did.

JEFF: You didn't turn the taps right off again.

DAD: Is that right, son?

JEFF: Every time I go for a shower, the taps are dripping. Now I know you don't turn them right off because you think you're saving the washers but, mate, I've told ya, that's what they're for, and I'm a plumber. I can change them. And a few flamin' washers are a damn sight cheaper than the water rates. It drives me mental, Dad. You know it does. If I've asked you once, I've asked you a thousand times, turn the fucking taps off!

DAD: Yes.

JEFF: Thanks.

DAD: Sorry.

JEFF: Very much.

DAD: I will try.

    JEFF walks out through the open kitchen door, and whips his towel off
    as he turns the corner of the doorway. DAD turns to the camera.

He's very wrought up. He only ever mentions that when he's wrought up. He must think he's meeting Mr Right tonight. He won't be eating any Sara Lee. You're probably wondering about that. About him meeting Mr Right.

    Well, may as well get it out into the open, as the actress said to the bishop. He won't be meeting any girl tonight, he's what you call, 'cheerful'. I can't bear that other word. Some of you will be going 'tut, tut, tut', I suppose. Can't see why though. He's a good, honest lad with a heart as big as Western Australia, and he's as much a friend as he is a son. He's a good mate. Mind you, he can be a nightmare to live with.

    JEFF's hands can be seen going through an open drawer of socks.

Come on, your dinner's on the table.

JEFF: You didn't do the laundry.

DAD: Sorry, I forgot.

JEFF: Yeah, well I need a pair of socks. I can't go bloody barefoot.

DAD: Well whiz down to the shop and buy yourself a pair of pantyhose.

JEFF: Hah, hah, hah. Very funny.

    JEFF sits on his bed and puts his socks on.

Suppose I can wash a pair and dry them in the oven.

DAD: Oh yeah, and the house will reek of burnt nylon like it did last time. Come and eat your dinner.

JEFF: Yeah, yeah. Two ticks.

DAD: [*to camera*] I wouldn't want you getting the wrong idea, though. Two blokes living alone together. It's only him. I'm not that way inclined. Bit of a lady's man, me. Always have been. When I was his age, I was a right little rooter, 'Rabbit' they called me. [*He laughs.*] 'Till I met his Mum, that is. No more fooling around after that. I was faithful to her from the day I met her. Because I knew I was one of the lucky ones. I knew it was love.

JEFF rushes in and stands in front of DAD.

JEFF: These jeans all right or should I wear the white ones?

DAD: How many pairs of my socks did you borrow? I can almost see your religion.

JEFF: Yeah, well, if you've got it, show it.

DAD: Haven't got that much to skite about.

JEFF: Well, Harry, size isn't everything, it's what you do with it that counts.

DAD: [*to camera*] His Mum always said that to me.

JEFF sits at the dining table with a dish cloth tucked around his neck.

What's that for? It's not spaghetti, you know?

JEFF: Don't want to get my new shirt dirty.

DAD: Have you actually met this young man? Or is there some young fella wandering around Sydney who doesn't know you're about to happen to him tonight?

JEFF: We've said 'g'day' a few times down the pub.

DAD: Ah. Courting?

JEFF: No, Dad. Not yet. But you never know your luck in a big city, though.

DAD laughs.

9. EXT. OUTSIDE/INSIDE DESIREE'S INTRODUCTION AGENCY – DAY

A tasteful sign indicates that Desiree's Introduction Agency will find you your Perfect Partner in Life. JOYCE JOHNSON, middle-aged, divorced, is sitting with her daughter JENNY, in JENNY's car, parked outside the agency. They've been there a while. JOYCE is twisting her handkerchief. JENNY is amused but tolerant of her mother's momentous decision.

JENNY: Are you sure about this, Mum?

JOYCE: No, Jenny, I'm not sure at all.

JENNY: Do you want me to come in with you?

JOYCE: No. This is something I've got to do. Now. Wish me luck.
JOYCE gets out of the car and enters Desiree's Introduction Agency. Once she looks back at JENNY who gives her a thumbs up, and then settles back to wait. Inside the agency MS ALLEN, calm and reassuring but wearing a lot of make-up, walks around JOYCE who is sitting in front of a computer. A SECRETARY clears the cups from the desk.
MS ALLEN: Now just relax, Mrs Johnson. I'm going to show you several faces. Now, I want you to just let them drift by. But if you see one that catches your eye, we can go back and have a second look.
JOYCE: Oh my God. Sorry. I'm a bit nervous.
MS ALLEN: Oh, no need to be, dear. You know, you've just taken your first step toward finding your perfect partner. Have a look.
MS ALLEN types on a few keys and a picture of a man with a moustache spins to a stop over the agency logo on the monitor screen. JOYCE, looking worried, watches MS ALLEN's hands typing. Another man spins to fill full screen of the monitor. MS ALLEN nods her head approvingly. JOYCE pulls a face. A picture of DAD fills the monitor screen. JOYCE smiles approvingly and nods.
DAD: [*voice over*] Yes, I'll give...

10. INT. KITCHEN. DAY.

DAD leans the telephone handset on his shoulder as he writes.

DAD: ...the party a call. Right. Yes, thanks very much. Thank you.
He puts the handset down and walks down the hallway and into the dining room. He resumes his seat at the dining table, across from JEFF.
JEFF: You eating or what? Who was that?
DAD: Man about a dog.
JEFF: What bloody dog?
JEFF squirts tomato sauce onto his plate. DAD is reading a book.
DAD: There's tomato sauce on it already.
JEFF: Yeah, I know. It needs more. Of course, some people don't think it's very good manners to read at the dinner table.

DAD: Some people haven't lived with you for twenty odd years.

JEFF: Some people should be so bloody lucky.

DAD: You should read a few more books, you know.

JEFF: Mmmm?

DAD: There's a lot more to life than what you see on telly. Like this bloke Sir Richard Burton, one of the greatest explorers that ever lived. First white man to see the Sacred Stone of Mecca, and the first man to discover the lakes in Africa that are the source of the Nile. A man -

JEFF: I thought he married Elizabeth Taylor?

DAD: ... who would take on the whole world, and conquer it.Not afraid of anything. You should read it, you might pick up a few hints.

JEFF: What for? I do not want to go chasing all over Africa looking for a place to have a swim. Anyway, the whole world has already been discovered.

DAD: No it hasn't.

JEFF: Which bits are missing?

DAD: There's amazing things waiting for you just around the corner, wonderful things like 'love, the greatest adventure of all', your grandmother said it once. I'll never forget it. 'The greatest explorers', she said, 'are the explorers of the human heart'.

JEFF: Is that why she became a dike?

DAD: Your grandmother was not a dike!

JEFF: She was licking Aunt Mary's pussy for forty years, what else do you call it?

DAD: I admit her relationship with Mary was... intimate... but she was not a *dike*! Lesbian, perhaps.

JEFF: Lezzo, dike, what's the diff?

DAD: What's the diff!? What's the diff!? Well, there's a hell of a lot of flamin' diff! Your Grandmother was a very beautiful woman, and just because she found happiness after your Grandfather died, just because, in her grief, she turned to Mary and the two of them found comfort in each other's arms, doesn't give you the right to call her names. How would you like it if I went around calling you 'pansy', 'fairy', 'poofter'?

22

JEFF: You do, half the time.

DAD: Only when I'm annoyed with you. Now eat your vegies.

JEFF: No, I've had it. I've done my dash.

DAD: Now you know...[*He sighs.*] You know how you get angry with me when I don't turn the taps off in the shower?

JEFF: Look, I'm sorry. It just gives me the shits.

DAD: [*interrupting*] No, no, no, no. Don't apologise. Listen, listen. Every time you finish a meal, you *always* push your plate away from you. Always. Now, I've told you until I'm blue in the face, but you always do it. It doesn't matter where we are. Here. Out. Buckingham Palace for all you care. You bloody do it and it drives me mental!

JEFF raises his arms in defeat and pulls his plate towards him.

JEFF: If that's how you feel.

They both laugh.

DAD: That's how I feel. There's a Sara Lee in the fridge.

JEFF: Mmm. No thanks, mate. Don't want to go breaking out in zits. Fact is, I'm running late as it is.

DAD: Bit early, isn't it?

JEFF: Well, you know what they say about the early bird.

DAD: Yes, but I don't think that's the sort of worm they had in mind when they said it. Ah, leave the dishes, I'll do them.

JEFF: Ta, Dad. I'll just clean my teeth.

JEFF walks away from the sink carrying the tea towel from around his neck and flicks it onto DAD's shoulder as he leaves the room.

DAD: [*to camera*] See what I mean? He hasn't been this excited for ages.

11. INT. GREG's HOUSE.

GREG is standing in front of his mirror, getting ready to go out. His MOTHER and FATHER are eating dinner at the kitchen table. GREG walks in and picks at some food on his plate as he walks to the kitchen.

FATHER: This one must be quite something. Your dinner's nearly cold.

GREG: Sorry.

FATHER: You might show some respect for your mother's cooking. Someone has to.

GREG: I'll grab something at the pub.

FATHER: Going out again, are we? Be nice if you spent some time at home occasionally.

GREG: It's Friday night, for Pete's sake.

FATHER: You smell like a Bombay brothel, too.

GREG: Good stuff that, Dad. 'Obsession', it's called. It cost a fortune.

FATHER: So where're you going? Dancing?

GREG: You never bloody let up, do you? I took dancing lessons to meet people, that's all. Wasn't as if it was ballet or anything.

FATHER: I only asked where you were going. And you watch your tongue in front of your mother.

GREG: Sorry, Mum. I'll see you later.

MOTHER: Be good, dear. Have a nice time.

FATHER: And if you can't be good, be careful.

> GREG goes.

See? I do try.

MOTHER: No you don't. You don't really try. You never give him an inch.

12. INT. DAD AND JEFF's HOUSE.

JEFF is standing at the bathroom mirror, checking his teeth which he rubs with his finger, then starts brushing them.

WOMAN ON TV: I was surprised by the amount of products that I had in my kitchen cupboard that were unfriendly. I'm also surprised at how harmful they were, the ones that I did have.

> DAD is reclining on a chair when JEFF walks in and stands beside the television set.

JEFF: You um, you don't feel like going out?

DAD: There's a film on telly. Don't worry, I'll watch it in my room. Coast will be clear.

JEFF: That's all right then. How do I look? God's gift?

DAD: Did you use a whole bottle of aftershave?

JEFF: Bit fierce, is it? 'Obsession'. He said it was his favourite.

DAD: Probably quite nice – in moderation.

> *JEFF goes to the bathroom and rubs the aftershave off from under his shirt with a face towel and starts to billow his shirt. DAD walks into the bathroom and hands him a towel.*

Where are you meeting him? At the Prinny?

JEFF: Yep. That's if he shows up.

DAD: I thought you had a date?

JEFF: Yeah, well, but you know. Knowing my luck.

DAD: There's plenty of others.

JEFF: No, Dad, this is different. He's something else. Nice.

DAD: Well, I expect he'll turn up then.

JEFF: Hope so.

> *JEFF walks out the front door followed by DAD. They walk along the porch.*

DAD: You've got to have more faith in yourself, Jeff. If you were my son's friend, you know, I'd be pleased it was you.

JEFF: Things don't always work out like that in the real world, Dad.

DAD: You'd better not keep him waiting.

JEFF: It's all right. Cop ya.

DAD: Bye. Have fun.

JEFF: Thanks, mate.

> *JEFF gets into his ute, loaded up with plumbing gear.*

Do me best.

DAD: [*to camera*] He's twenty-four years old and he's no virgin, that's a sure and certain fact... but he's carrying on like it was his first ever date. You might have noticed that he lacks a bit of confidence about himself in the romantic stakes. Can't think why, he's a nice enough looking lad, if you like that sort of thing, but about three years ago a terrible thing happened to him – he fell in love. It didn't last that long, the other bloke, Kevin, I think it was, he was a nice enough lad, but a bit flighty, training to be a Qantas steward, or something. And after about three months, he just moved on to greener pastures, and it just about broke Jeff's heart.

13. INT. NIGHT. JEFF'S UTE.

JEFF is driving the ute.

JEFF: [*to camera*] It's true. Grandma was a dike. Well, lesbian. I used to go and stay down there for my holidays, you know. They were the best times.

14. B & W FOOTAGE. INT. GRAN'S HOUSE.

GRAN and young *JEFF praying. They smile at one another and* young *JEFF* climbs *into bed. GRAN tucks him in and kisses his forehead.*

JEFF: [*voice over*] Just a little brick and tile down by the Hawkesbury, nothing flash, but clean. Gran was always polishing every bit of woodwork in the house. So you'd get up in the morning and there'd be this wonderful smell of lavender floor polish all over the place.

15. EXT. JEFF DRIVING – NIGHT.

JEFF: ...It reminds me of a funny story. S'pose it's a bit off..

16. B & W FOOTAGE: YOUNG JEFF IN BED.

JEFF: [*voice over*] I was there once, some of my cousins were staying too. So I had to sleep in the spare bed in Gran's room, you know ... I remember ... I could see it so clearly: waking up that first morning, looking across to Gran's big old double bed ...[*GRAN and MARY are lying in the brass bed, fast asleep, wrapped up in each other's arms.*] ... and there were Gran and Mary, tucked up in bed, wrapped up in each other's arms. Gran was snoring, I remember. I lay there looking at them for such a long time. Just looked natural, somehow, you know? Like the most natural thing I'd ever seen. Like love.

17. INT. DAD AND JEFF's HOUSE.

DAD picks up the telephone and starts to dial a number. JENNY walks to the phone and picks it up in JOYCE's apartment.

JENNY: Hello?

DAD: Joyce Johnson?

JENNY: No, no. I'll just get her.

    JOYCE is sitting reading a book.

    Mum, it's for you.

JOYCE: [*into telephone*] Hello?

DAD: [*into telephone*] Ah, look. You don't know me, but my name's Harry Mitchell. I got your name from Desiree's Introduction Agency.

JOYCE: Oh, yes. Mr Mitchell. Pleased to meet you.

DAD: Please, call me Harry.

JOYCE: Of course... I'm sorry, Harry, but uh -

DAD: Look, it's all right. It's the first time I've done this sort of thing, too.

JOYCE: Oh, you mean you don't use Desiree's on a regular basis?

DAD: No! No, nothing like that. No, I'm interested in a serious relationship and the most important thing to me is companionship. I was thinking that we should meet, have a meal, you know, somewhere quiet, classy. Um, I happen to be a member of the Rozelle Leagues Club.

JOYCE: Isn't that a bit rowdy?

DAD: Well, they have a very nice dining room actually, and there's dancing. Proper dancing. Oh, but if, you know, if you'd prefer a movie or races or whatever.

JOYCE: Oh, no, no, no. I'd like to have dinner at your club.

DAD: You would?

JOYCE: Mmmm.

DAD: Oh, that's very nice, Joyce. Well then I'll pick you up on Saturday. Say half past twelve?

JOYCE: Or I could meet you there if you like, Harry?

DAD: No, no. No. It would be my pleasure. I'm looking forward to it. I promise.

JOYCE: Me too.

DAD: 'Till Saturday, then.

JOYCE: 'Bye.

DAD: 'Bye then.

18. INT. THE PRINNY BAR.

PATRONS in the Prinny Bar. Loud music and general hub-bub. JEFF enters and looks around. He walks up to the bar where a PATRON looks him up and down. GREG is drinking a beer at another bar. JEFF waves to catch GREG's attention and gestures with his hands to go outside. GREG looks over his shoulder and shows nervousness. They walk into the poolroom of the bar and past GEORGE and other PLAYERS, into the beer garden.

GEORGE: G'day, Baxter.

JEFF: Hi, George, [*To Greg*] That's better. Couldn't hear myself think in there. Cheers.

GREG: Yeah, cheers.

They drink their beers.

Baxter?

JEFF: Oh, it's a joke. The footy team, you know.

JEFF and GREG together: Baxter the walls boys, here comes Jeff.

They laugh and begin to feel more relaxed.

GREG: So, you play footy?

JEFF: Just the local pub, just amateur. Bit of a laugh.

GREG: It's more than a laugh from what I've heard. What goes on in those locker rooms?

JEFF: Oh, it's a man's world, mate. It's all spit on the floor and 'how many sheilas did you root last night?' Do you play any sport?

GREG: Yeah. Swimming. I do a lot of swimming. Keeps me away from home a fair bit, I suppose that's why. All by yourself, in the water. No one to hassle you, give you a hard time, you know. Won a few medals too, at school.

JEFF: Wouldn't mind seeing you in your Speedos.

GREG: Well, I'll show you later. Got them on now. If you'll wear your footy shorts.

JEFF: You're on.

> *They leave the pub and cross the street. JEFF leans on a wire fence as he talks to GREG.*

I really liked you from the first time I saw you down the pub. It took me yonks to pluck up the courage to even say 'g'day'.

GREG: I thought you weren't interested, you know. I've seen you too, in the park. I work in the park. And I've seen you there, jogging, in your footy gear. Those shorts look really sexy on you.

JEFF: What you said before – about home – don't you get on at home?

GREG: Oh, Mum's all right, but Dad's a bit tricky, you know. He's always picking on me, finding fault with everything I do. He went through the roof when I got my job.

JEFF: Gardening? What's wrong with that?

GREG: He said it wasn't good enough for me. No future in it. But I'm bringing home nearly as much money as him, already. He's – I don't know, he's like a stranger to me. Someone I live with but don't know very well and don't like very much. That's why I took up swimming.

JEFF: Things are a little bit different at our house.

> *He touches GREG's cheek.*

Do you want to come home?

> *GREG nods and JEFF does too.*

19. EXT/INT. DAD AND JEFF's HOUSE. NIGHT.

JEFF's ute pulls up in front of the house with two wheels on the footpath. JEFF and GREG get out and walk to the gate. Inside, DAD is lying in bed, reading.

JEFF: Just push it open.

> *They go into the house. JEFF closes the door behind them.*

Make yourself comfy. Want a beer?

GREG: Where's ah... Is your Dad out?

JEFF: He'll be in bed.

GREG: [*whispering*] Well, shouldn't we be a bit quiet then?

JEFF: [*whispering*] What for?

GREG: [*whispering*] In case we wake him up.

JEFF: Hah. He won't be asleep. Not yet. Probably come and say 'G'day' and see who's here. I told you, he knows all about me. What I do and who I do it with. I bring blokes back all the time. [*Hastily*] Not that there's that many. I mean – I should be so lucky. What I'm trying to say is that Dad knows and he doesn't care.

GREG: Well, if you're sure?

JEFF: Scouts honour. If they've got any left.

> *The sit on the lounge.*

Come on. Sit down. Relax. That's better. Cheers.

GREG: Yeah, cheers.

JEFF: I'm really glad you showed up.

GREG: So, what about the other teams? The football teams.

JEFF: You're just an old footy perv, aren't you?

GREG: Uh huh.

JEFF: Just 'coz they're big, butch footballers, doesn't mean they're Superman in bed, you know. Every year, the team goes to Manila, for a, you know, post season holiday, and every year they end up in a brothel. We've got this one real prick with ears, Jack Rhymer, first time he was really shocked. He'd been with this Asian chick, she was all over him, you know, done everything, like a Chinese gymnast. Jacko wasn't too keen on that. He said he kept wishing he was with an Aussie girl, who'd just lie there like a soggy cornflake.

GREG: What do you like?

JEFF: Well, I dunno as I'd win any gold medals, but I like a bit of action.

GREG: So do I.

> *JEFF draws closer and kisses GREG. They embrace and continue kissing.*

DAD enters from his room.

DAD: Don't let me interrupt anything.

GREG jumps from JEFF's hold, rushes to a shelf and leans on it, looking embarrassed.

JEFF: [*huskily*] For crying out loud, Dad. Can't you ever knock?

DAD: I was just going to get myself a beer. Anyone else?

JEFF shakes his head impatiently and DAD walks out of the room. GREG, finding something to do, plays with the ship propped on the buffet. JEFF rushes up to him.

JEFF: It's okay. I promise you. Relax, just carry on as usual.

GREG: But he saw us.

JEFF: Oh fuck, he's seen worse than that. A couple of years ago, I had a friend who stayed the night. We were having a wake up session, Dad brings the tea right in the middle of it.

GREG: What did he say?

JEFF: He said 'careful of the sheets'. It broke the ice.

DAD, with a can of beer in his hand, walks back into the room.

DAD: Well, aren't you going to introduce me?

JEFF: Yes, sorry. Uh, this is Greg. Greg, this is my Dad.

DAD: Very pleased to meet you. You can call me Harry. Sit down.

GREG: Thanks.

DAD sits on the lounge and pats the seat next to him.

DAD: Make yourself at home.

GREG: Thanks.

GREG sits awkwardly next to DAD. He slides over closer to DAD as JEFF motions him to move over. JEFF sits next to GREG, trapping him between himself and DAD. DAD raises his beer and so does GREG.

DAD: Well, up your bum.

GREG splutters.

JEFF: It's just a joke. Dad's always making jokes.

DAD: Yeah, like that time with the lavender floor polish -

JEFF: Steady on, Dad. It's a bit off, that is.

DAD: Is it?

JEFF: In company.

THE SUM OF US

GREG: What was that about lavender floor polish?

JEFF: Oh, don't worry about it. You wouldn't be interested. It's just a misunderstanding.

DAD: What do you do for a crust, son?

JEFF: He's a gardener, Dad.

DAD: Oh yeah. Deaf and dumb, is he too?

GREG: I work at the Botanical Gardens.

DAD: Is that right? Perhaps the young fella would like another drink.

GREG: Oh.

JEFF: Want something stronger?

GREG: No, no. This is fine.

JEFF: Got some scotch, maybe a drop of brandy left?

GREG: Wouldn't say no to a drop of scotch. You know what they say: 'whisky makes you frisky'.

JEFF: And 'brandy makes you randy'.

DAD: Hey, pity we don't have any rum, eh?
They all laugh.

GREG: That's a good one, I like that.

JEFF: I'll make a double then, I'll just get the ice.
JEFF leaves the room to get ice from the freezer and begins preparing drinks. He turns to watch as DAD and GREG walk out the back door.

20. EXT. BACKYARD. NIGHT.

GREG and DAD are examining the tomato plants.

GREG: These are wonderful.

DAD: My pride and joy. Not as good as my brother, Eric's. I don't know what he does.

GREG: Well, you know what they say about tomatoes. Same as lemon trees.
They continue to talk as they urinate on the tomato plants.

DAD: Busy at the Prinny?

GREG: Yeah. It was packed.

DAD: Nice pub.

GREG: What, you've been there?

DAD: Oh yeah. Well, you know, when it became obvious that Jeff was, well that way – I thought, well, his heart, his life and I'd never met any willie woofters, so I – sorry – gay persons and – not that I knew of, anyway, I thought 'well I've gotta find out what this is all about'. So I got him to take me on a pub crawl. Started off at the Prinny.

21. B & W FOOTAGE. INT. PRINNY BAR.

JEFF and DAD toast each other with their beers.

DAD: [voice over] ... We had a great old time. I had no idea there were that many places. We ended up at The Barracks, I think it was.

22. INT. BARRACKS DANCE FLOOR.

A DANCER performs. DAD is drinking beer with two men. He isn't properly dressed for it and looks out of place, but is having a grand time. JEFF dances with the CROWD on the dance floor.

DAD: [voice over] I got talking to a couple of blokes, you know, a bit nancy, but really a lot of fun. And one of them, he must have thought I was that way inclined, he asked me my name and when I said 'Harry', he said 'Oh no, that doesn't suit you at all. You'll always be Harriet to me'. Well, 'Harriet' is not a name I've ever been fond of, so I said, 'Harriet, never! Call me Henrietta!'

23. EXT. BACKYARD. NIGHT.

GREG can't believe his ears.

GREG: 'Henrietta', eh? It doesn't really suit you.

DAD: Eh? You reckon? I thought it was pretty good, meself. I mean, a bit refined, you know?

GREG: Cripes. I just can't imagine my Dad...

DAD walks further into the back yard and GREG follows. JEFF rushes out of the back door, pausing at the doorway to fix the fly on his jeans. He stops at the bottom of the stairs and listens to DAD's laugh. DAD and GREG are sitting on the swing behind the house.

...ever doing something like that.

DAD: What's that?

JEFF walks over to the swing and hands GREG a scotch.

GREG: Cheers.

DAD: So, you live at home, uh?

JEFF: Greg.

GREG: Yeah. Worse luck.

DAD: And uh, you don't get along with your family then ... Greg?

GREG: Well –

JEFF: Greg's folks don't know about him yet, Dad.

DAD: I see. Don't you think that's a shame, Greg?

JEFF: Leave it, Dad.

DAD: I've always been very grateful for Jeff being honest with me. I mean not that I had a lot of choice, finding him in the back shed there when he was – what – fourteen, were you? You know, sticking it up Willie Jones' bum.

JEFF: I was not up his –

DAD: Well, near as bloody damn it, mate.

GREG: You are very broad minded, Mr Mitchell.

DAD: I try to be, mate. I have to be, you know. I mean this is Jeff's home and if he's unable to be himself here, where can he be? And I want you to think of this as your home too, eh, Greg? You're welcome here any time you like. We don't have any secrets from each other here.

JEFF: Nothing on telly, Dad?

DAD: Nothing worth watching. This is much better, eh?

GREG: Well, up your bum, Henrietta.

DAD: Up your dress, Griselda.

JEFF: You two are well away, aren't ya?

DAD: Tell me, what's your ambition? You know, what's your dream – apart from playing Hide the Sausage with young Jeffrey here? I mean, what would you like to do in life?

GREG: My secret dream? My really, truly secret dream? I'd really like to plant a forest, you know? To plant a whole forest and watch it grow, and go and stand in the middle of all these great trees and say, 'I planted this, I made this'.

DAD: That's magnificent. Do it. That's wonderful, don't you think, Jeff?

JEFF: Bloody oath. Make a fair old swag of violins too, wouldn't it?

DAD: 'Make a fair old swag of violins too'. Don't you have any respect for the English language?

JEFF: What's wrong with the way I talk?

GREG: I like the way he talks. It's real manly. It turns me on. I'm sorry, Harry, that was a bit bold.

DAD: Please, pretend I'm not here.

JEFF: Yes, please.

DAD: Why don't you get the young fella another whisky Jeff?

GREG: No, no really. I'm a two pot screamer.

JEFF: I'm a bit like that, myself. Two, and I'm anybody's.

GREG: Three, and I'm everybody's.

DAD: Four, and I'm nobody's.

GREG: Actually, maybe I will have one more. I might do anything.

JEFF: Feel free.

> JEFF takes GREG's glass and leaves him and DAD sitting on the swing.
> Then they too, follow JEFF inside.

GREG: Nice place you've got here, Harry.

24. INT. JEFF'S BEDROOM.

DAD *walks into the room followed by* GREG. *He puts his hand on* GREG's *shoulder, directs him to the bed and sits him down.*

DAD: I'm very pleased you like my boy, Greg. He doesn't push himself very much, eh – sometimes, but he's got a heart of gold, and he likes you.

GREG: Well, I think he's very nice.

DAD goes to the cupboard and comes back carrying some magazines and sits beside GREG.

DAD: But if you need anything to, uh, well uh, he can be a bit of a lump. I've got these magazines, you know, if you need anything to get started.

GREG: Um, well uh, are these Jeff's?

DAD: Yeah. No. I bought them. I just wanted to find out what sort of thing he got up to. I had a fair idea, of course, but there's some things in here that I would never'd imagined. And this one, it's about safe sex. I was worried about this terrible AIDS thing. I mean, who isn't these days? And I just wanted to find out if Jeff was safe. Well, you know, it worries me, he's my son. So I thought I'd just leave these lying around so that Jeff could find out what it was about, but he told me that he knew...

GREG: It's all right, Mr Mitchell, I do safe sex too, if that's what you're worried about.

They both stand. DAD shakes GREG's hand.

DAD: Well, there you go then. If you need a turn-on. Well, have a good time, won't you?

GREG: Thanks.

DAD: Yeah. I'll get out of your way now. It's been very nice to meet you, Gary.

GREG: Greg. You too, Mr Mitchell.

DAD: Don't do anything I wouldn't do, you two.

DAD pauses in the doorway then walks into the kitchen as JEFF returns with more drinks.

JEFF: Can't believe he's gone. I thought he'd never get the hint.

25. INT. JEFF's BEDROOM.

JEFF and GREG are on the bed and JEFF begins kissing GREG'S neck. GREG

THE SUM OF US

begins to undo JEFF's *buttons. They are embracing and kissing each other. The door opens and* DAD's *face appears.*

DAD: Ah – Sorry. Greg, I forgot to ask, how do you take your tea in the morning?

GREG: As it comes.

DAD: White with two?

JEFF: Piss off, will ya?

DAD: Don't mind me. Night all.

> DAD *closes the door behind him.* GREG *leans back onto the pillow as* JEFF *is leaning over him on the bed.*

JEFF: He really does mean well. Where was I?

GREG: Look. Do you mind. I think I'll give it a miss.

JEFF: Come on. It's still early.

GREG: No, really. Another time.

JEFF: Did he say something to you?

GREG: No. No. He's a wonderful man. It's just... I've got a bit of a headache, you know.

JEFF: I've got some Panadeine.

GREG: Doesn't help. Migraine, you know.

> GREG *begins putting his shirt on.*

I need those really strong ones. I better push off.

JEFF: It's him,. isn't it? It's Dad.

GREG: No. It's not him. It's not you or anyone. It's just me. I can't hack it. Bringing your boyfriend home and not having to lie and pretend. Look, I think it's really terrific what you've got with him, I really do.

JEFF: But –

GREG: It hurts a bit. It makes me feel guilty about what we do. Maybe it's too domestic. Sort of makes the atmosphere – I dunno – not very sexy. I'd like to see you again, Jeff, I really would. I like you a lot, you're a really nice guy, so's your Dad. Tell him I say 'goodbye'.

> GREG *leaves. Tears come to* JEFF's *eyes.*

26. EXT. FRONT PORCH. NIGHT.

JEFF runs out of the front door and stands on the porch. GREG *is standing at the top of the stairs. He looks up at* JEFF.

JEFF: Don't go, mate. Please. I like you, mate, you know. I don't just mean sex, we don't have to do that if you'd rather not. I like you as a person, you know. I feel comfy with you. Just don't go, please. We can talk, get to know each other a bit.

    He pauses.

    I'm wasting my breath, aren't I?

GREG: Yeah, sorry.

JEFF: No. I'm sorry.

GREG: Well, I'll see you then?

JEFF: Yeah, of course.

GREG: I *do* like you, Jeff.

JEFF: Ta.

    GREG *turns and walks away.* JEFF *watches him from the front door. He walks inside and closes the door.*

27. INT. KITCHEN.

JEFF is holding a drink, leaning against the kitchen counter.

28. B & W FOOTAGE. INT. TRAIN.

JEFF: [*to camera*] I went down to Melbourne once. Kevin had moved there and I thought...

    In a train carriage, a woman wearing too much make-up is sitting holding a drink.

    ... I thought I could talk him into getting back with me, you know. Didn't work, of course. The point is, I went down by train, and there was this woman. Couldn't take my eyes off her. Suddenly she said:

WOMAN: Oh. The agonising pain of it all. The agonising pain.

The WOMAN *stands up from her seat and staggers away, dropping the glass onto the table next to the seat.*

29. INT. KITCHEN.

JEFF, *holding his drink, is still leaning on the kitchen counter.*

JEFF: 'Oh, the agonising pain of it all', that's what she said. I've often wondered what she meant, but I suppose I knew straight away. She just wanted someone to talk to. Someone to laugh with, have a good time with, get drunk with, cuddle up to. Doesn't seem a lot to ask, does it?
  JEFF *grabs the bottle of scotch, carries it and his drink to the kitchen table, sits and slams the bottle and drink onto the table.*
I mean, for fuck's sake, how can you be too bloody domestic?

30. INT. DAD'S BEDROOM.

DAD *is lying in bed, reading. The television is next to the dressing table. We see* DAD'S *reflection, in bed, in the mirror.* DAD *closes his book and puts it beside him on the bed.*

MALE TV VOICE: Sensational value at two thirty nine. It's part of a new range that includes a two and a half seater, a sleeper sofa version, and you can buy matching chairs. We have all of them now in stock.

31. EXT. BACK VERANDAH. NIGHT.

DAD *walks into the kitchen, through to the back room and out the back door. His feet stop at a bottle of scotch whisky sitting on the back stairs. He sees* JEFF *sitting cross-legged on the ground, leaning against the clothes line and drinking out of his glass.* DAD *leans down, picks up the bottle and continues down the stairs.* JEFF *holds up his empty glass.* DAD *pours him another glass of straight scotch.*

DAD: He seemed like such a nice lad, too.

JEFF: Yeah. Didn't he.

DAD: Are you seeing him again? Plenty more fish in the sea, eh? I was wondering what you'd like for tea tomorrow night. Thought I'd buy a leg of lamb. You always like a roast, I'll make baked potatoes, thick gravy and um, don't forget to sort out your laundry. I'll get it done for you tomorrow. You ever thought of going to a – an introduction agency? One of those computer dating services. They've got them in those magazines of yours.

JEFF: Not tonight, Dad. Some other time maybe.

DAD: Fair enough. Don't stay up too late, will you, son?

JEFF: No, Dad.

> DAD *turns and makes his way up the back stairs into the house.*

[*to camera*] She comes into my mind from time to time. That woman on the train.

> *JEFF takes a sip from his glass and looks up thoughtfully.*

32. EXT. CAR PARK. DAY.

DAD drives into a car park overlooking the beach. He parks and gets out of the car wearing a suit and holding a bouquet of flowers. He adjusts his tie and slicks his eyebrows and smiles at his reflection in the car window.

33. INT. JOYCE's FLAT. DAY.

A reflection of JOYCE checking herself in the mirror. The front door buzzer sounds. She has one last look in the mirror before turning to the front door where DAD's shape can be seen through the translucent glass door. She opens the door.

DAD: Joyce?

JOYCE: Mr Mitchell.

DAD: Please...

> *He offers the bouquet of flowers he had hidden behind his back.*

41

...call me Harry.

JOYCE: Ah. That's very thoughtful.

> *She takes the flowers and sniffs them.* DAD, *still standing at the doorway, raises his eyebrows.*

34. EXT. TROTTING RACETRACK. NIGHT.

Racetrack lights are on. Trotting horses with their carriages are on the racetrack. DAD *and* JOYCE *are in a grandstand, cheering the horses on.* DAD *leans over and gives her a kiss on the cheek. They are all smiles.*

35. EXT. FISH RESTAURANT. DAY.

The sun shines and water sparkles in the background. A bottle of wine is on the table. DAD *breaks open a crab from a seafood platter for a smiling* JOYCE. *He takes the crab meat out and puts it on her plate.*

36. INT. JOYCE's APARTMENT.

JOYCE *is talking happily into the phone.*

37. INT. DAD's FERRY.

DAD *in the cockpit of his ferry, is talking with mobile phone to his ear. He is smiling.*

38. INT. JOYCE's APARTMENT.

JOYCE *in her apartment, smiling and talking on the phone.*

39. EXT. BEACH PROMENADE. DAY.

They walk along the beachside together, eating icecream.

40. INT. FERRY CABIN. DAY.

JOYCE is driving the ferry under DAD's instruction. DAD leans around and over her so that he traps her between himself and the wheel which she is holding. He winks at the camera, gives JOYCE a kiss on the cheek, then leans his cheek against hers.

41. INT. LEAGUES CLUB. NIGHT.

Everyone is dressed to kill. DAD is playing the poker machines. Dials spin and stop on a win of two aces. JOYCE walks around the side of the poker machine to join DAD.

JOYCE: Harry, look at you. You're on a winning streak.
DAD: Ever since I met you, Joyce. You look wonderful.
JOYCE: I must say, you always know the right thing to say to a woman.
DAD: Life without women would be like a barbecue without beer, wouldn't it? Speaking of which, shall we go? I've reserved our usual table.

42. EXT. BEACH. DAY.

JENNY and JOYCE are lying on their stomachs on the grass, overlooking the beach. A couple stroll by on the footpath.

JOYCE: I haven't had so much fun in ages.
JENNY: This is getting a bit serious, isn't it, Mum?
JOYCE: No. No. It's just fun to go out again, with someone you like, who obviously likes you.
JENNY: Mum.
JOYCE: It's all right, dear. Harry's great but we'll take it step by step. I'm a bit more wary these days.
JENNY: Hey, look. Dad left you, it wasn't your fault.

JOYCE: Well, of course it was, part of it. You can't put all the blame on one side when a marriage breaks down.

JENNY: Would you ever take him back?

JOYCE: No, dear. Never. Once bitten and all that.

43. EXT. BACKYARD. DAY.

DAD's car is parked outside the house, two wheels on the footpath. There is washing on the clothes line. DAD walks out of the back door, down the stairs and stops. JEFF is smoking a joint, sitting on the swing. He offers DAD the joint, but he declines.

DAD: Ahem.

JEFF: Not much else to do, is there?

DAD: Sitting around here all the time, feeling sorry for yourself, getting stoned. You should be out looking at the world, making a contribution. Sowing your oats. Something wonderful, like love, the greatest adventure of all. Your Gran said it once.

JEFF: I make a contribution, mate. I look after people's drains. You know life would be pretty shitty without plumbers.
He laughs morosely.

DAD: Not very romantic though, is it? I mean, not like planting a forest.

JEFF: Fair go, mate. I'm just me.

DAD: I know you are. You have that freedom. So go on, prove to me that the way I brought you up wasn't wrong. That my mother wasn't wrong. That what she found was wonderful, that it was worth everything: all for love. That young Gary, he seemed keen enough.

JEFF: Greg. Greg. Don't start Dad. Not now. Just go and have some fun. You got some rich widow you're seeing on the sly, have ya?

DAD: What if I have? You're not the only one that gets lonely, son. I like women. I like the way they're put together. I like them all... soft and squishy. I like having them, for Pete's sake. I'm sick of living in sin with my own right hand.

JEFF: Ease off, Dad.

DAD: Oh, that shouldn't worry you, should it? You're going for world champion wanker, aren't you?

JEFF: [*to camera*] Sorry about that, he got a bit carried away or something, I dunno. I mean it's not quite like that. I mean I do it. Of course I do, who doesn't? Got to relieve the tension somehow. But he makes it sound like I'm some sort of rampant sex maniac. You don't like to think of your own Dad doing that, do you? I mean, you know he must. Doesn't seem quite right, does it?

44. EXT. BACKYARD. DAY.

DAD walks out the front door, closes it, and walks along the porch. He stops, holding onto the railing.

DAD: [*to camera*] He drives me screaming up the wall sometimes. It's not an easy thing for a man to accept that his mother's been doing it with another woman for forty years.

    DAD steps down to his car parked on the footpath, opens the driver's door and pauses.

[*to camera*] I used to wonder that the love between them must be extraordinary if they're prepared to risk everything, all for love. That's when I started to think about blokes and blokes. Never did it, of course. Never wanted to. I think it was the idea of the hairy bums that put me off.

45. EXT. OUTSIDE JOYCE's PLACE. DAY.

DAD drives into the car park outside JOYCE's place by the beach.

DAD: [*to camera*] But if what Mum and Mary had was so amazing, well I thought maybe it's the same for men too. Anyway, I met my wife, then there was Jeff. Then I thought 'ah well, it's in the blood'. It's just skipped a generation, you know, from my mother to him.

    DAD gets out of the car and puts his coat on.

And I made up my mind that no matter what, that he'd be his own man, and I knew that I'd love him. But he drives me screaming up the wall sometimes.

46. EXT. OUTSIDE CLUB. NIGHT.

DAD and JOYCE emerge from the club and stroll together. They pause at the Step Fountain in Darling Harbour.

JOYCE: This has all been a bit of a shock to me, Harry. Us getting on so well. It's a nice shock, I might add. I didn't have very high hopes when I went to that agency. I never expected anything – serious.

DAD: It is, on my part.

JOYCE: How serious?

DAD: I want you to meet Jeff, then if the two of you get on, I'm going to pop the question.

JOYCE: And um, if we don't?

DAD: We'll cross that bridge when we come to it.

JOYCE: Woah. I wouldn't want to come between you two anyway. You seem very close.

DAD: We've got to think of ourselves first, Joyce.

JOYCE: It's a big step all the same. But I guess we should put our cards on the table. Look, I might not be very imaginative in the bed department, Harry, but I never said no to my husband, not in all the years we were married.

DAD: Not once?

JOYCE: Well, obviously there were certain times after Jenny was born, and when I wasn't well, but no, apart from that, he always got his onions, whenever he wanted them. Could have had them a bit more often, too, if he played his cards right. I like to be wooed.

DAD: Yes. You do, don't you?

JOYCE: So, as long as you're not too demanding, you'll get what you want on that score.

DAD: I think we should stop beating around the bush, Joyce.

JOYCE: I didn't think I was.

DAD: Well, you don't have to give me your answer straight away, but you know what's on my mind.

DAD bends down onto one knee and takes JOYCE's hand.

Will you marry me?

JOYCE starts to cry.

What's all this? What's this all about? Eh? What's the matter?

JOYCE: I'd given up hope. I just didn't think it was going to happen to me again.

DAD: No, neither did I.

JOYCE: I've been so lonely for so long and I just didn't think – It's *you*, kneeling down that did it.

DAD: Well, will you?

JOYCE: No.

DAD: Why? I thought -

JOYCE: It's too soon. I don't want to make another mistake. Look, let's give it six months and then if we still feel the same way -

DAD: Make it three months.

JOYCE: [*laughing*] It's all that talk about sex, isn't it? It's got you all worked up. All right, three months.

DAD: Joyce. Mmmmm mmmm I can't say I'm the happiest I've been in my life, but I'm the happiest I can remember being for a very long time.

DAD leans over to JOYCE and they kiss.

47. EXT. BALMAIN MARKETS. DAY.

A plastic Santa Claus is displayed on one of the stalls as DAD and JEFF walk through the Balmain markets. JEFF stops at a stall with boxer shorts and holds them up to DAD.

JEFF: Yeah, mate. Mate, that's you. That is you. Look at that. You can't wear Y-fronts all your life, mate.

DAD walks away as JEFF pays the stall holder for the shorts. They stop and look at a stall of animals in cages. A WOMAN is cradling a duck.

There is a stuffed wallaby wearing a Santa hat.

They go to the pub. JEFF *is sitting on the pub balcony with lunch on two plates in front of him.* DAD *joins him carrying tomato sauce and two schooners of beer.* JEFF *takes the bottle of tomato sauce and squirts it onto each of their plates.*

Back at the markets, there is a SANTA *with Christmas trees.* DAD *and* JEFF *go to have a look at the trees as* SANTA *walks away with one.*

DAD: Too small.

JEFF: What's got into you this year? That's twice the size that we normally have.

DAD: We don't make enough of Christmas, that's our trouble. It's the season of good will. Family. It's high time you started thinking about a family of your own. Find some nice young fella, get set up in life.

JEFF: It's not that flamin' easy. Doesn't just happen to order. The choice is a bit more limited for one thing. Maybe some places like San Fransisco, all the blokes wear their dicks on their sleeves, they reckon.

DAD: You ever thought of going there for a holiday?

JEFF: I don't want to live like that, Dad. I don't want to live in a world that just begins and ends with being gay. I like having all sorts of people around: kids and old folks, every sort of person there is. I don't want to live in a world without women. I like women. Me and the girls in the office get on great. They know and they don't care. We laugh about it. Fancy the same blokes sometimes. Even fancied a couple of the girls. Done it with a few of them just to make sure I wasn't missing out on anything.

DAD suddenly pokes his head out from behind the Christmas trees.

DAD: You've done it with girls? You never told me that.

JEFF: Yeah. I didn't want you to get your hopes up.

DAD: Did you like it?

JEFF: See what I mean?

JEFF turns away. DAD *reaches out his arm and taps* JEFF *on the shoulder.*

DAD: Hey, hey. Bugger it. Could you get it up?

JEFF: Of course I could. It's not exactly an obstacle course. I quite enjoyed it actually. Something different. But they just don't turn me on like men do.

DAD: Would, would you like to try it again?

JEFF: No, Dad. Not off the top of my head. See what I mean about getting your hopes up? I like doing it with blokes, Dad. I don't think that's ever going to change because I don't want it to. I don't want to be limited by other people's ideas of who I am. Yours or anyone else's.

DAD: I don't think I've ever put any limits on you, Jeff.

JEFF: No. Dad, I know. You've been great, mate. The best Dad in the world, I reckon. Fairest, that's a certain fact. I don't often say it, but it's Christmas, so thanks, mate, for everything. You give me the first class shits at times, and I suppose I do you, but I don't think there's many got a father like you.

DAD and JEFF embrace.

DAD: And I'm a very lucky man to have a son like you, mate.

DAD looks up at a pine tree. There is a church steeple in the background.
What do you reckon?

JEFF: How are we going to get the fucker home?

48. EXT. CAR. DAY.

DAD is driving the car up the street with a huge Christmas tree strapped to the roof. Tree branches cover the windscreen.

49. INT. SITTING ROOM. DAY.

JEFF is decorating the tree with Christmas lights. DAD enters the room carrying a fairy doll.

DAD: Magnificent. Just what Christmas should be. Ta da.

JEFF: Not her again. I thought we were going to ditch the bitch.

DAD: Never! Your mother bought her the first Christmas of our marriage, just before you were born. I suppose some people might see that as an omen.

JEFF: She's looking a bit tacky, Dad. Why can't we get a nice star or something?

DAD: Not as long as I'm alive. You can do what you like when I'm gone. Your mother loved her.

JEFF: I miss her, Dad. I miss her like crazy.

DAD: Not half as much as I do, lad. It's not possible.

JEFF: Yeah, mate, I know. I'm sorry.

DAD: I think about her sometimes. Sitting on a fluffy white cloud in a place called 'Paradise', surrounded by lots of fat little naked babies sprouting wings. [*He laughs.*] And angels playing harps, making pretty music. Waiting for me to come along and join her. It helps, sometimes. Sometimes it makes it worse. Sometimes I miss her so much, I can hardly wait to hear the pretty music.

JEFF: Come on Dad. Cheer up, you old piss head. Give me a hand.

DAD: Yeah, well, you know.

JEFF: You should take a leaf out of your own book, mate. I mean, there's bound to be a few old widows floating around.

DAD: There's a few young ones too.

JEFF: Yeah, but I mean within the realms of possibility, mate. Somebody who'll fancy you.

DAD: Would it worry you if there was?

JEFF: Hell, no, it'd be great.

DAD: Well, there is.

JEFF: What? You old dog. How long has this been going on?

DAD: A while.

JEFF: You are lower than a snake's belly, you know that? Not a single word to me about this.

DAD: Now don't go getting all hurt. I just wanted to be sure.

JEFF: Calls for a celebration?

DAD: I'll drink to that.

50. EXT. DAY. GARDEN.

JEFF hands DAD a champagne glass and pours beer into both their glasses.

JEFF: So, um, have you um, have you stuck it up her yet?

DAD: You dirty bastard! You bastard! Don't you dare -

JEFF: You have, haven't you? Is that where you've been all these nights?

DAD: Listen, don't you talk about Joyce like that, if you don't mind. She's a very refined kind of person.

JEFF: So is it love then, Dad?

DAD: No. Well, I can't honestly say that it is. But it might be the next best thing.

JEFF: [*smirking*] Cheers.

> DAD *and* JEFF *drink their beer from the champagne glasses in one gulp.* JEFF *refills them.*

So, when's it going to be?

DAD: Well, we haven't set the big day.

JEFF: But you're going to?

DAD: Yeah. I, you know, if she gets on with you.

JEFF: I do not come into this. Unless you need me to move out, or anything.

DAD: Of course I don't, Jeff. And nor would Joyce want that. No, she knows about you.

JEFF: Yeah? You haven't told her everything, have you, Dad?

DAD: Well, no. I mean, not that. Not yet.

JEFF: Dad.

DAD: Well look, Joyce is a very kind and understanding woman. You'll love her and she will love you. And you know, when things work out, because they will, well you can stay here in your own home, as long as you like, until such time as you want to move out, on your own or with someone.

JEFF: Well I'll be ... huh?

DAD: Merry Christmas, son.

JEFF: Come here, you old bastard.

> *Under the clothes line* JEFF *embraces his father and pats him on the back.*

Merry Christmas, Dad.

51. EXT/INT: DAD AND JEFF's HOUSE. NIGHT.

DAD opens the front door. JOYCE is standing on the porch, smiling. She holds up a bottle wrapped in red with a big gold ribbon. They kiss.

DAD: Joyce. Happy New Year.

JOYCE: Happy New Year, Harry.

JOYCE: Um, aren't you going to shut the door.
> *They laugh.*

DAD: Sorry.
> *JOYCE hands DAD the bottle. She walks in, stops and picks up a framed photograph.*

JOYCE: Ah. Is this Jeff?

DAD: Yes. On his twenty-first.

JOYCE: Oh, takes after his Dad, in the looks department.

DAD: Do you reckon? Some people say they can't see the resemblance.

JOYCE: I find that difficult to believe.
> *DAD and JOYCE embrace and kiss.*

Um, I'm really hanging out for a drink.

DAD: Make yourself at home.
> *He goes to prepare the drinks. JOYCE wanders about, looking at things.*

JOYCE: Jeff's out on the town tonight?

DAD: Too right. New Year's Eve. Don't expect him home till the morning.

JOYCE: This is really pleasant out here, Harry.

DAD: You sound surprised.

JOYCE: Oh well, you know, two blokes living together, you keep it really nice and tidy.
> *JOYCE notices the gay magazines. She picks one up and flicks it open.*

Oh! What are these doing here?

DAD: To be honest, I bought them.

JOYCE: What? Why?

DAD: Well, Jeff's uh -

JOYCE: Oh. I see. Why didn't you tell me?

DAD: I was going to. I know I should've.

JOYCE: You bought these?! You encourage him?! Jesus, you ought to be ashamed of yourself. You ought to be ashamed of yourself.

JOYCE throws the magazine onto the ground in disgust and walks out of the room. DAD follows her with a sigh. She is standing on the porch, shaken. DAD approaches her.

DAD: I've never been ashamed of Jeff. Not ever. How can I be ashamed of what my seed's become? What my love's become.

JOYCE: You couldn't tell me. I mean it's probably the most important thing in your life, and you couldn't tell me.

DAD: It doesn't change anything.

JOYCE: Well it does to me. All this time I've been thinking I've been getting to know you, you've been lying to me.

DAD: I never actually lied.

JOYCE: It amounts to the same thing.

DAD follows JOYCE along the porch as she speaks. She is fighting back tears. She goes to her car and opens the door.

DAD: Just meet Jeff. You'll love him. You'll see.

JOYCE: Harry, no. I can't. Not now. It's not just him anyway, it's everything. I can't.

JOYCE gets into the driver's seat of the car.

DAD: Joyce.

JOYCE: I just need to be on my own for a bit. Sort things out in my head. It was good for a while there, Harry. If only you'd been honest.

JOYCE starts up the car. DAD watches it drive away.

DAD: [*to camera*] Ashamed of Jeff. Never. Disappointed? Yeah, that he'll never give me a grandchild, disappointed that I honestly believe he'd be missing out on something wonderful. What I had with his Mum, making a baby, knowing that I'd put the seed in there and watching it grow, then seeing him. But if he's never going to have that, then I want him to have all the things he can have. Our children are only the sum of us. What we add up to: us and our parents and our grandparents and theirs. All the generations.

52. B & W FOOTAGE. EXT. DAY

The back of a car can be seen driving along a path through the bush.

53. EXT. NIGHT. STREET OUTSIDE THE HOUSE.

DAD hears explosions, turns his head and looks up to the sky to see the fireworks.

54. B & W FOOTAGE. EXT. GRAN's PORCH. DAY.

GRAN kisses MARY on the cheek. They are holding hands. GRAN has tears in her eyes. MARY, with arms outstretched, is also crying.

55. EXT. FIREWORKS EXPLODING. STREET OUTSIDE THE HOUSE. NIGHT.

DAD is looking up at the sky. His eyes close and clench as his hand comes up and clutches at his heart. His face is contorted with pain. His eyes start to roll back. He begins to fall. As his face hits the ground fireworks explode in the sky.

56. INT. HOSPITAL.

Medical meter and dial and breath monitoring bag in glass container are arranged beside DAD's hospital bed. JEFF is sitting beside him, watching his face. DAD opens his eyes. JEFF starts to get teary.

JEFF: Hi, mate. They said you'd be with us soon. What'd you go and do a silly, bloody thing like that for? You've had a bit of a stroke, Dad. Well, it was more'n a bit of one, actually. Did they tell you what it was going to be like? You'll be all right mate. I'll look after you, no sweat. Things'll be just the same as always, Dad, I promise.

DAD moves his hand, but JEFF doesn't notice. JEFF looks behind him.
Can I get you anything? Need to go for a wee or something? Silly eh?
Suppose they look after that sort of thing here. But still, you never
know.
    *JEFF notices DAD's hand moving. Then he puts his hand on DAD's right
hand.*
Why do you keep moving your hand? Can you hear me?
    DAD touches JEFF's hand with his left hand. JEFF watches.
Once for 'yes'.
    JEFF looks from DAD's face to the hands. He looks from DAD's face to the
hands.
Twice for 'no'.
    *Two fingers of DAD's hand touch JEFF's hand twice. JEFF leans down
and cries on DAD's hand. DAD closes his eyes. He leans forward and
cries harder like a lost child.*
Oh, Dad.

57. EXT. BOTANIC GARDENS. DAY.

*GREG, in gardening uniform, is washing his hands in a sink. The HEAD
GARDENER and GARDENERS walk along a path talking among themselves.
They come around a corner and walk towards GREG at the sink. MIKE and the
HEAD GARDENER stop in front of GREG who turns to face them.*

HEAD GARDENER: Are you knocking off early?
GREG: What do you mean, it's five past.
HEAD GARDENER: What are you, a bloody clock watcher now? I thought
    you might give us a few minutes extra, considering that cock-up you
    made with that bed of pansies last week.
    *The HEAD GARDENER walks away, blowing GREG a kiss and revealing
MIKE still washing his hands.*
MIKE: He's a prick. Don't take any notice.
GREG: Water off a duck's back.
    GREG and MIKE play fight.

MIKE: You're in a good mood. You piss off. I'll put your gear away.
GREG: Thanks, Mike.

58. EXT. BOTANIC GARDENS. DAY.

GREG runs down the path beside the Garden Centre.

59. INT. GAY BAR. NIGHT.

A DRAG QUEEN adjusts a bustier over her breasts and fixes her headgear. A CROWD OF PATRONS is happily drinking. GREG and two friends wearing scarves and cowboy hats are practising a dance routine observed by WALTER, the waiter.
WALTER: Great boys! Is there going to be a rodeo later?
GREG: Hey, why don't you come with us Walter? Come with us.
WALTER: Love to.
GREG: Marty! Marty, we'll see you there. See you down there.

60. EXT. TAYLOR SQUARE, SYDNEY. NIGHT.

The Mardi Gras Parade is coming along the street which has been closed to traffic. A huge, friendly crowd watches from the sidelines as the floats and bands and dancing people in amazing costumes proceed along the parade route.

61. INT. GREG'S HOUSE. NIGHT.

The Gay and Lesbian Mardi Gras is on the television screen in GREG's home.

MALE TV REPORTER: Police estimate tonight's crowd to be over six
hundred thousand...
    *FATHER is reading a newspaper. He tilts it down to see the TV and
    resumes reading the paper. MOTHER sits on the lounge, shaking her
    head in amazement. FATHER, looking over his newspaper, shakes his*

head in distaste.
This is believed to be the largest crowd ever to gather for the annual Gay and Lesbian Mardi Gras.

On the television screen GREG appears, dancing on a float, wearing a scarf around his neck, no shirt and cowboy pants and hat. Two other DANCERS turn and dance past him revealing that they are wearing G-strings. GREG dances towards them and takes over the TV screen.

MOTHER blinks in disbelief. FATHER looks up from his paper at the TV and sees GREG holding up a toy gun to the camera. FATHER drops the newspaper onto his lap in shock. MOTHER swallows, there is a lump in her throat. On TV, GREG is in his element, blowing imaginary smoke from the barrel of his toy gun. Tears appear in FATHER's eyes.

62. EXT/INT. GREG'S HOUSE. DAY.

GREG gets out of a taxi outside his house. The taxi drives off as GREG walks to the side of the house. He pushes the sliding door open and enters, closing the door as quietly as possible. He tiptoes into the kitchen where his MOTHER is at the stove.

GREG: Mum, what are you doing up?
    MOTHER shakes her head at him. His father walks into the kitchen and up to GREG.
FATHER: You're late. What have you been doing? What were you doing? You were all over the late news.
GREG: I was having a good time with my mates.
FATHER: I ought to beat the shit out of you.
GREG: Well, why don't you try?
FATHER: Get out! Get out of here now. You can come back here once for your things, when I'm not here. Then that's it. I never want to see you again.
MOTHER: He doesn't mean it, Gregory. He's angry.
GREG: No. He does, Mum.

FATHER: Damn right, I do.

GREG: Fair enough.

> *GREG turns and walks out. MOTHER stares after him, tears in her eyes. She shakes her head.*

63. EXT/INT. DAD AND JEFF'S HOUSE. DAY.

JEFF pushes an empty wheelchair through the hallway into DAD's room and beside DAD on his bed. He leans forward and reaches for a switch on the arm of the wheelchair. It buzzes on each press.

JEFF: Here you go, Dad. I fixed it up a treat, mate. Now we can talk to each other, sort of. What do you think? It's good, isn't it?

> *DAD, lying on his bed, rolls his eyes. He taps his fingers on his left hand.*

No, it's not silly, mate. It's good. It works well. Now, we're having an outing this arvo. Taking you down to the supermarket. Pick up a nice bit of fish for your tea, some of that frozen lasagna you like so much. Here's your remote. Do you want it on?

> *JEFF holds the remote control up and switches on the TV. The mirror in the background reflects DAD lying in bed watching. He rolls his eyes.*

What about your wee pan? Need a piss? Come on, Harry, now you know you're not going to be able to piss in the supermarket. I'll just go and get us ready. Back in a tick.

> *JEFF walks around the wheelchair and out of the room. DAD sits up and crosses his arms.*

DAD:[*to camera*] The trouble with having a stroke is that people treat you like a fuckwit afterwards.

64. INT. SUPERMARKET. DAY.

DAD, in the wheelchair, is wearing headphones as JEFF pushes him through the supermarket. GREG is shopping as well. They should meet, but they don't. They keep missing each other in the maze of aisles, but DAD spots GREG and finds a use for the buzzer. He buzzes furiously. JEFF sees GREG and smacks DAD's shoulder as he wheels him away. He takes the earphones off and leans down to DAD's ear.

JEFF: Shut up, Dad. Don't make a row.
> *A woman shopper pushes her trolley past DAD and JEFF. DAD looks at his son, then at the camera, eyes to heaven – it is a battle of wills between JEFF and his paralysed DAD. DAD is carrying a basket of groceries on his lap and it drops to the floor. JEFF leans down to pick it up as DAD's chair hits a display. The cans cascade off the shelf and crash to the ground. GREG, reaching for butter on the dairy shelf, turns his head. JEFF quickly collects his groceries from the ground as DAD looks up at GREG. JEFF pauses and looks up.*

GREG: Jeff... g'day... thought it was you.
JEFF: G'day, Greg.
> *GREG crouches and helps JEFF put the groceries back in the basket.*

GREG: How're you going Mr Mitchell? Not too good by the looks of things.
JEFF: Dad's had a bit of a stroke.
GREG: Yeah, I heard, down the pub.
JEFF: He can't speak or nothin', but he knows it's you.
GREG: How can you tell?
JEFF: I just can. So how're things?
GREG: Oh, not bad. I've left home.
JEFF: Your folks?
GREG: Mum's been great, but Dad. Found a place of my own, actually. A studio flat, they call it. It's quite nice but it's hardly enough room to swing a cat and it's pretty expensive.
JEFF: I would've thought you'd have found some nice friend to move in with.
GREG: I wish. I, you know, I do meet blokes but they're all only after one thing. That's not everything in life, is it?
JEFF: Can't understand it.
> *DAD rolls his eyes then frowns.*

Look, we better push off, I've to get Dad home.

GREG: Yes, of course. I'll see you later, Mr Mitchell. Hope you're feeling better soon.

JEFF: Yeah, thanks, Greg.

GREG: Listen, I might drop around one night, make sure he's looking after you properly.

JEFF: Probably be a bit difficult.

GREG: Oh well, if you don't want to see me.

JEFF: No, it's just, you know, a bit difficult with Dad.

GREG: You've got to have a life of your own, surely.

> DAD *starts buzzing.*

JEFF: Yeah, of course I do. Dad, Dad, Dad. Yeah, of course I do. It's just, you know, when he's a bit better, eh?

GREG: Yeah.

JEFF: Tooroo.

GREG: See ya later.

65. INT. KITCHEN. DAY.

JEFF, wearing an apron, is preparing food in a blender. He hears the doorbell and turns his head, spilling some of the food.

JEFF: Yeah, two ticks!

> *Taking off his apron,* JEFF *opens the front door.*

No, sorry. Don't want any.

JOYCE: Jeff.

66. EXT/INT. DAD AND JEFF'S HOUSE. DAY.

JOYCE is standing on the porch at the front door. She is holding a bouquet of flowers. JENNY *sits, waiting in the car in the background.*

JOYCE: My name's Joyce Johnson. I'm a friend of your Dad's.

JEFF: Joyce. Yeah. Sorry, come in.

JOYCE: How is he?

JEFF: As well as can be expected, you know. Um. Doc says he can never walk again. He can't speak, of course. Do you want to see him?

JOYCE: Ohh. I didn't realise it was that bad.

JEFF: He'd be pleased to see you.

JEFF walks into DAD's room, followed by JOYCE, still holding the flowers.
Dad, someone to see ya.

JOYCE: Harry? I'm so sorry to hear about your, about your being sick.

JEFF: Oh, he's not sick now. Look, I'll leave you two alone so you can have a chat.

JOYCE: Look, it's all right. I just dropped by.

JEFF walks up to her, ignoring her plea, and takes the bouquet from her hands.

JEFF: I'll make a cup of tea.

He leaves the room. JOYCE approaches the bed and gently sits on the edge of it. She reaches for his hand and holds it.

JOYCE: I'm really sorry, Harry.

67. INT. KITCHEN.

JEFF at the kitchen table is preparing a pot of tea. JOYCE walks into the kitchen.

JEFF: Tea's ready.

JOYCE: Look, I won't stay. My daughter, Jenny, she's waiting for me. Bit of a shock seeing him like that. He used to be so full of energy.

JEFF: Hah. Still is. Always wanting to go down the park for a walk, walk down the shops – wheel, I should say.

JOYCE: Must be difficult for you.

JEFF: Nah. Got a nurse, comes in three times a week and it's me Dad, you know. Look, drop in again sometime. He likes visitors.

A tear drops from JOYCE's eye and she turns away.
Sorry I gave you such a hard time before, I thought you were one of them missionaries, we get a lot of them around here. When it's blokes like the Mormons, I just open the door, tell them I'm a poofter and

watch them blush.

JOYCE: You tell them what?

JEFF: I'm a poofter. Didn't he tell you? Yeah, he was going to, he was a bit worried about how you might react.

JOYCE: No, I knew. You're nothing like I expected.

JEFF: Real sweet on you, he was. Had his heart set on you.

68. EXT. STREET. DAY.

JOYCE walks across the road to the car where JENNY is waiting for her. She is holding back her tears.

JENNY: How was it? Are you okay?

JOYCE: [*teary*] Ohh. There's no fool like an old fool. Isn't that what they say?

JENNY: You're not so old, Mum.

DAD's bedroom window can be seen in the background.

JOYCE: No. But I'm a fool.

JOYCE is holding back her crying with difficulty. JENNY puts her seat belt on, looking at her mother with concern. They drive off.

DAD: [*to camera*] My mother was eighty, she was getting infirm and Mary was a bit younger...

69. B & W FOOTAGE. INT/EXT. GRAN AND MARY'S HOUSE.

MARY and GRAN are sitting on the edge of their bed.

DAD: [*voice over*] ...but neither of them could look after each other any more...

GRAN and MARY are crying. GRAN leans over and kisses MARY on the cheek.

...and we all made the decision to split them up. My brother took Mum, and Mary ... went to a home. It was for their own good. How many times did we tell ourselves that?

Dad's brother, Eric, his wife and DAD *enter the room and take* GRAN *and* MARY.

...We drove Mum away and she didn't say a word. She didn't speak for days, she just...

Eric's wife holds onto MARY *as* MARY *grips onto* GRAN's *hand.* ERIC *holds onto* GRAN's *other hand while* DAD *follows behind.* MARY *is crying inconsolably.*

...sat in her new bedroom with her suitcase full of memories. She died in her sleep one night, not long after that. And I never had the chance...

Eric's wife assists MARY *as she is led to a waiting nurse, around the corner of the porch.* DAD, ERIC *and* GRAN *watch.* MARY *grips* GRAN's *hand.*

...or the guts to ask her the one thing I wanted to know. I always wanted to know what they said to each other that last night, lying there in that great old brass bed, knowing it was for the last time, knowing that they were never going to see each other again, knowing they were being taken away to different places to die...

MARY *is crying, her arm outstretched towards* GRAN.

...I can't imagine...

MARY's *and* GRAN's *hands are stretched, clutching to one another.*

...what they would have said. How do you say 'thank you' for forty years of love? What words could you possibly find? By then, they were both as deaf as posts, so did they lie there shouting their love and their goodbyes to each other?

Eric places a suitcase into the boot of the car as his wife gets into the front passenger seat. DAD *holds onto* GRAN's *arm and reaches for the back door.* MARY, *held by the* NURSE, *waves to* GRAN. *She starts crying once more as the car engine starts.*

...Did they find comfort in the idea that they might meet again soon, in the next world?

GRAN *looks out the back window of the car and waves as the car drives off.*

So, I don't know what I would have said to Jeffrey if I'd known the stroke was going to happen. I know I would have said something. Only now I'll never know what it was.

70. INT. DAD'S ROOM.

JEFF wheels DAD's chair into his room.

JEFF: Okay, Dad. Time for number twos. I'll be back in a bit to wipe your bum. Got the fish on for tea, right?
>*JEFF walks away toward the kitchen leaving DAD on the toilet.*

DAD: [*to camera*] I used to imagine, in my darker moments, that it'd be the other way round. That he'd catch that dreadful disease and I'd be the one nursing him to the grave. But not this. Dear God, anything but this. Oh, maybe in a few years' time, when I'm gone, he'll find someone, even if it's out of sheer bloody loneliness. But it won't be love, because by then he'll have forgotten how. I can't imagine anything worse could happen to a human being than that. [*Farts*] Sorry. It always used to be a very private thing for me, going to the lav. Not any more.

71. EXT. BOTANIC GARDENS. DAY.

JEFF wheels DAD around the corner of a path in the Sydney Botanic Gardens, along the path beside the pool, then to a seat under a tree.

JEFF: Ripper of a day, isn't it? Weather report said it was going to rain. They still don't get it right very often, do they? Might get an ice cream on the way home. Do you fancy an ice cream?
>*DAD buzzes once as JEFF locks the brakes on the wheelchair.*

Don't suppose you'd manage an iceblock, not unless I chopped it up for ya. Might be a bit messy.
>*JEFF crouches to eye level with DAD. He looks over DAD's shoulder and sees GREG planting flowers.*

You need a wee or anything, Dad?

DAD buzzes twice.

Well, I do. You'll be right, Dad. I won't be long
  JEFF walks over and stops a short distance from GREG, who is still crouched planting flowers. GREG looks up.

GREG: G'day.

JEFF: Fancy meeting you here.

GREG: I'm planting.

JEFF: What?

GREG: I'm –

JEFF: Yeah, yeah. I know. I saw you from over there. Well, I wasn't actually sure it was you, I was just having a perv. Nice legs.

GREG: You're looking pretty fit yourself.

JEFF: No, no. I need some sun. At least you've got a tan.

GREG: It's only my arms and legs. The rest of me is as white as a ghost.

JEFF: Looks all right to me. You didn't come and see Dad.

GREG: Well, I didn't think you wanted me to.

JEFF: Yeah. Sorry I was a bit off last time I saw you but, I wasn't sure how you'd react to Dad, you know, it's not the most romantic thing in the world, is it? Looking after your father after he's had a stroke. I thought you might think it was too domestic. [*He smiles.*] Look, the thing is um, I'd really like to see you again.
  They stare at each other.

72. EXT. BOTANIC GARDENS. DAY.

JEFF runs up to DAD.

JEFF: You right then, Dad? I'll read to you for a bit, eh? Do you want me to read to you?
  DAD buzzes twice.

No? What do you want to do? Sit here and listen to the flowers grow?
  DAD buzzes once.

All right. Sorry I was a while, but I ran into young Greg. You probably remember him best as Gary. Could've knocked me down

with a feather. But I suppose it's only natural, him being a gardener and this being a garden. Couldn't help myself. I asked him over for tea one night. I was thinking he'd say: 'Oh yeah', and that'd be that. Could've knocked me down with a feather when he said 'would tomorrow be all right?'. 'Yeah, ripper' I said. [*He laughs.*] I was a bit worried about you. How he'd feel about you. But he just shrugged and said 'well, that's life, isn't it?' And he said he'd bring his toothbrush. Now that's making it fairly plain, isn't it? He might even stay the night. I'm not going to rush things though. Joe Cool this time, you just watch me. Not too cool though, I don't want him to think I'm not interested, you know. I'm just gonna be – me. Who ever that is.

He laughs. DAD *squints. He has tears in his eyes.* JEFF *notices.*

What's up, Dad? What's the matter, mate, you're crying. Hey? What's wrong? Hey, come on. It can't be that bad, whatever it is. Come on, it's all right, dry your eyes. Come on...

JEFF cuddles DAD *and presses his face against* DAD*'s head.*

Oh, don't, Dad. Please. It breaks me up to see you like this, you know it does. There's nothing to get upset about, mate. I'm here. I'll always be here. Okay?

DAD *buzzes four times.*

Is it Greg?

DAD *buzzes twice.*

Don't you want him to come to tea?

DAD *buzzes a few more times.*

I won't. I'll stop him if you want me to. I've got his number.

DAD *frustrated, continues to buzz a few more times.* JEFF *stops him from continually buzzing.*

Is that it? Dad, come on? Dad, Dad, Dad, Dad, come on, tell me. One buzz is for yes, two buzzes for no.

DAD *buzzes once.*

Yes, you want me to cancel.

DAD *rolls his eyes, lets out a sigh and buzzes twice.* JEFF *is smiling.*

No, you don't want me to?

DAD buzzes once. JEFF smiles with relief and cuddles his father.
Yes?! That's what I thought. You all right? You sure? Silly old bugger, getting yourself worked up over things, eh? Nothing to worry about, Dad. I promise. Not a worry in the world.
[*To camera*] Turned out real nice after all, didn't it?
DAD is smiling.
[*Concerned*] I wonder if he'll show up.
DAD rolls his eyes to heaven.

73. EXT. AERIAL SHOT. DAY. END CREDITS OVER SHOT.

JEFF pushes DAD away through the park. The Sydney skyline is before them, bright and light, with the Botanic Gardens, the opera house, ferries on the water of the harbour, and in the distance the commercial docks of Balmain.

THE END

Film Credits

Harry Mitchell JACK THOMPSON/Jeff Mitchell RUSSELL CROWE/Greg JOHN POLSON/Joyce Johnson DEBORAH KENNEDY/Young Jeff HOSS MORONEY/Gran MITCH MATHEWS/Mary JULIE HERBERT/ Football Coach DES JAMES/Footballer MICK CAMPBELL/Ferry Captain DONNY MUNTZ/Barmaid JAN ADELE/Jenny REBEKAH ELMALOGLOU/Desiree LOLA NIXON/Greg's Mother SALLY CAHILL/ Greg's Father BOB BAINES/George PAUL FREEMAN/Barman WALTER KENNARD/Leather Men STUART CAMPBELL GRAHAM DRAKE/ Woman On Train ELAINE LEE/Gardener ROSS ANDERSON/Foreman MICHAEL BURGESS/Dad's Brother JOHN RHALL/Brother's Wife HELEN WILLIAMS/Nurse JAN MERRIMAN

Production Manager ANNE BRUNING/First Assistant Director CAROLYNNE CUNNINGHAM/Art Director IAN GRACE/Sound Recordist LEO SULLIVAN/Continuity JO WEEKS/Costume Supervisor LOUISE SPARGO/Make-Up Supervisor LESLEY ROUVRAY/Carnera Operator KATHRYN MILLISS/Focus Puller LEILANI HANNAH/ Clapper Loader JOSE KEYS/Camera Attachment JONATHON PASVOLSKY/Gaffer IAN (FLOWERS) PLUMMER/Best Boy ROBBIE BURR/First Electrics GRANT ATKINSON/Key Grip SIMON QUAIFE/Grip DAVID HANSEN/ Boom Swinger SUE KERR/Production Co-Ordinator JULE SIMMS/ Production Secretary ELLY BRADBURY/Production Accountant MICHELE D'ARCEY/Assistant to Hal McElroy BRONWEN STOKES/ Assistant to Kevin Dowling CAROL PRUGH/Production Runner SIMON COX/Second Assistant Director HENRY OSBORNE/Third Assistant Director GUY CAMPBELL/Unit Manager WILL MATTHEWS/Assistant Unit Managers LAURE

PETTINARI DENNIS HULM/Unit Assistants GREYDEN LE
BRETOR ANDREW MARSHALL/Locations TRANSIENT
IMAGES/ Wardrobe Co-ordinator LYN ASKEW/Wardrobe Standby
GABBY DUNN/ Wardrobe Assistant KELLY MAY/Make-up
Assistant ADELE WILCOX/Set Decorator KERRIE BROWN/Set
Dresser FAITH ROBINSON/Standby Props TOM
CHURCHILL-BROWN/Art Department Assistant JONATHON
TIDBALL/Draughtsman MARTIN TREVOR/Construction Manager
GEOFF HOWE/Carpenters EUGENE LAND STEVEN TULLOCH
AIDAN PAUL CARTWRIGHT/Scenic Artist NICK WALKER/Set
Painter ZENNA BLEWITT/Construction Runner TIM HIGGINS/

Publicist VICTORIA BUCHAN/Stills Photographer JIMMY
POZARIK/ Caterer LERRY FETZER/Catering Assistants VICTORIA
CONANT KAY RICKERBY/Jack Thompson's Standin JOHN
RHALL/Russell Crowe's Stand-in GLENN FOLPP/Safety GEORGE
MANNIX BERNIE LEDGER/Casting Assistant SARAH
KANTS/Constultant RICHARD BARRETT/Financial Controller
PETER ANDERSON/Business Affairs Manager VICTORIA
SHERNGRAM/Financial Assistant SANDRA WAINE/Associate
Editor SHAWN SEET/Assistant Editor LINI HARRISON/Additional
Assistants JANE MAGUIRE DANIELLE WIESSNER/Editing
Facilities SPECTRUM FILMS/Sound Effects JOHN PATTERSON
HELEN BROWN/Foley JOHN DENNISON ROSS BREWER
CRAIG BUTTERS/Dialogue TONY VACCHER ROSS
BREWER/Sound Assistant CRAIG BUTTERS/Liaison MARY
DENNISON/Mixing JOHN DENNISON TONY VACCHER/
Sound Post Production AUDIO LOC SOUND DESIGN/Music
Production CHARLES FISHER for MINUTE
PRODUCTIONS/Mixing/Engineering CHARLES FISHER JIM
BONNEFOND/Music Supervisor JOHN HOPKINS for
SCREENSONG/ "Sister Madly" and 'Better be Home Soon" (Neil
Finn) Mushroom Music, performed by Crowded House courtesy of
Capitol Records and EMI Music Australia/"Can We Get Closer"

(Diesel)Lizard Songs/EMI Songs Australia performed by Diesel,
courtesy of EMI Music Australia/"Ain't That The Way" (Dave
Faulkner) performed by Formula One, featuring Tina Harrod produced
by Charles Fisher/"Will I With You" (Gyan) Trafalgar Music,
performed by Gyan courtesy of Trafalgar Records, produced by Charles
Fisher/"Sh-Boom" (Feaster/Keys/McRae/Edwards) ©1954 Hill & Range
Songs & J. Albert & Son performed by The Chords, courtesy of
Atlantic Recording Corp. by arrangement with Warner Special
Projects/"It Will Be Alright" (Jimmy Barnes/Jell Neill) Dirty Sheet
Music/EMI Songs Australia/ Mushroom Music performed by Jimmy
Barnes, courtesy of Mushroom Records/"Frozen In Time" (Dave
Faulkner) performed by Dave Faulkner, produced by Charles
Fisher/"Rockin' Christmas" (Jim Mangle/Glen A Baker) Mushroom
Music, performed by Ol '55 courtesy of Mushroom Records, produced
by Charles Fisher/"Sh-Boom"(Feaster/Keys/McRae/Edwards) ©1954
Hill & Range Songs & J Albert & Son performed by Margaret Urlich,
courtesy of Sony Music Australia arranged by John Stuart, produced by
Charles Fisher/ "Love Explosion" (Dave Faulkner) performed by
Formula One, featuring Tina Harrod produced by Charles Fisher/"The
One and Only You" (Mark Seymour/ Hunters & Collectors)Hurnan
Frailty/Mushroom Music performed by Hunters & Collectors, courtesy
of Mushroom Records/"I've Learned to Cope" (Maxwell/Ferris/Russell)
Sony Music Publishing Australia/Warner Bros. Music/ Mushroom
Recordsperformed by Bass Callute, courtesy of Mushroom Records/
Soundtrack available on Picture This Records/Laboratory
ATLAB/Laboratory Liaison DENISE WOLFSON/Negative Matcher
LAREM PSALTIS BRIAN JAMIESON/ Grading ARTHUR
CAMBRIDGE/opticals ROGER COWLAND/Titles EXTRO
DESIGN OPTICAL & GRAPHIC/Camera Equipment
SAMUELSONS FILM SERVICE/Completion Bond FILM FINANCE
INC/Insurances H W Wood Australia/Legals HEIDTMAN & CO/
The producers wish to thank: NEIL BALNAVES/ LEICHARDT
MUNICIPAL COUNCIL/THE BUCCANEERS RLFC/TIM
VINCENT/ Eastman Film System by KODAK/Developed in

FILM CREDITS

Association With THE GREAT SUM FILM LIMITED PARTNERSHIP/ International Sales SOUTHERN STAR FILM SALES/
This film is the subject of copyright. No part of this film may be reproduced or transmitted In any form or by any means without the written permissionof the owners except where permitted by law. Any unauthorised copy, duplication or presentation will result in civil and criminal prosecution./The characters and events portrayed in this programme are fictitous, and any relation to any person, living or dead, is purely co-incidental./ All rights reserved./©1994 Australian Film Finance Corporation Limited/Southern Star Entertainment Pty Limited.SPAA Registration No 0437

Resource Materials

A video of the film *The Sum of Us* is available, released by Southern Star Entertainment in Sydney.

A resource booklet for students and teachers of English, film and media studies is published by Currency Press: *Why study a film script? – The Sum of Us as text* by Su Langker, teacher of English and the Media at Sydney Boys' High School.

Orders to Currency Press, P.O. Box 452, Paddington, NSW 2021, Australia. Tel. (02) 332 1300 Fax. (02) 332 3848